Water Babies

By Gina Ingoglia

Illustrated by Lisa Bonforte

A GOLDEN BOOK • NEW YORK
Western Publishing Company, Inc., Racine, Wisconsin 53404

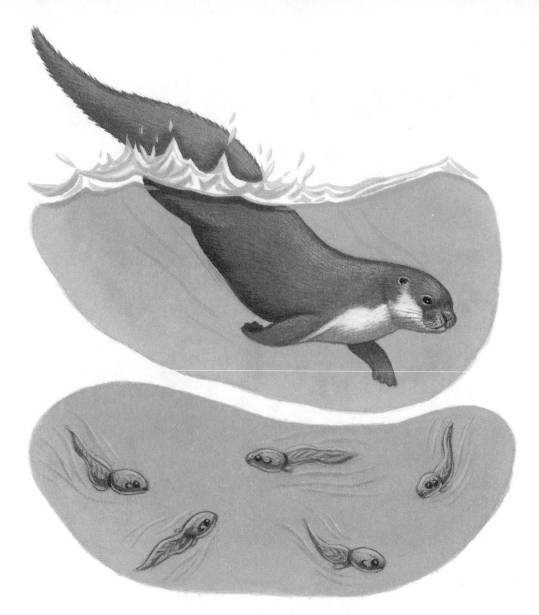

Many baby animals love the water. Some are born underwater and never come ashore. Others are born on land but spend most of their lives in the water.

These animal water babies can be found in
rivers, streams, lakes, and oceans. In some parts
of the world the water is freezing cold. In other
places it may be as warm as bathwater. But
wherever they live, these baby animals feel at
home in the water—and they are all wonderful
swimmers!

GRAY SEAL

Baby gray seals can swim shortly after they are born. Even when the water is cold, their soft white fur keeps them cozy and warm. Instead of legs, they have flippers that help them swim very fast. Baby seals like to take naps and dry off on rocks that have been warmed by the sun.

PORPOISE

Baby porpoises live in oceans and rivers.
When they are born, they are almost half as long
as their mothers! Their slippery, smooth bodies
are shaped to move very fast through the water.
These babies often leap into the air as they
swim. This is called "porpoising."

PENGUIN

Most baby penguins live where the weather is cold and snowy. Although they are birds, they can't fly. They have powerful flippers instead of wings.

When penguins are just a few months old,
their waterproof feathers have grown in, and
they are ready to swim. The young birds stand
together at the edge of the water. At first the
penguins don't seem to want to get wet, and
there's a lot of pushing. But once they jump in,
the young penguins are fine swimmers. They
paddle very fast with their flippers, especially
when they swim underwater.

POLAR BEAR

Polar bears are born in caves made of ice and snow. They stay inside for several months with their mothers. When the little bears finally leave the cave, it is still too cold to go swimming.

However, in the springtime, when the ice breaks up, the bears get their first swimming lessons. If their thick fur gets too heavy with water and weighs them down, their mothers help them stay afloat. But someday the little polar bears will be big and strong enough to swim for miles and miles on their own.

RIVER OTTER

Baby river otters love to play! They slide down slippery mud banks and chase one another in the water. They are very good swimmers and learn to dive by copying the older otters. By the time river otters are only eight months old, they can take care of themselves.

HIPPOPOTAMUS

Little hippos live where the weather is sunny and hot. They are usually born underwater and spend their days in the rivers, swimming or just trying to stay cool. When baby hippos swim, it looks as if they are walking in the water.

FROG

Many kinds of baby frogs hatch from eggs that are laid in the water. At first the hatchlings don't look like frogs. They look like tiny wiggling fish and are called tadpoles. Weeks go by and the tadpoles change shape. Their tails disappear and legs begin to grow. Slowly the tadpoles become little frogs. Then the little frogs swim fast with their long, strong legs.

DUCK

As soon as baby ducks are hatched on land,
they follow their mother right into the water.
They swim close behind her wherever she goes.
Baby ducks eat small water plants and insects.
They suck up the water with their strong tongues.
Then they strain out the food with their bills.

GREEN TURTLE

At night, baby green turtles are hatched from eggs that have been buried by their mother on a beach. Then the little turtles quickly scramble out of the sand and into the warm water. Soon they have swum far out to sea.

Females will return to shore years later to lay
eggs of their own. Males will probably stay at
sea for the rest of their lives.

CROCODILE

As soon as baby crocodiles are hatched, their mother picks them up in her mouth and carries them into the water. The little crocodiles are able to swim right away. They like to eat small shellfish and tadpoles.

BROWN PELICAN

The brown pelican baby eats fish that its mother and father have already eaten! The food is brought back up and the baby reaches down into its parents' throats to get the fish. The young bird learns how to fish and swim and dive by copying its mother and father. The stretchy "bag" that hangs under its bill is called a pouch. It's used for storing fish.

BEAVER

Baby beavers are born inside a lodge made of mud, branches, and leaves. When beavers are about six weeks old, they ride on their mother's back as she swims. But they learn very quickly how to swim alone.

Baby beavers can swim fast because they have webbed feet and broad, flat tails. Their front paws are like hands and are often used to carry things around in the water.

SEA HORSE

Baby sea horses are born from eggs that their mother lays in a pouch on their father's belly. The pouch is like a big pocket and the eggs are kept safe inside. When they hatch, baby sea horses are less than one inch long.

These unusual little fish swim by bobbing up and down as if they are standing up. They often rest by holding on to seaweed with their curly tails.

OCTOPUS

Octopus babies are very shy and hide among underwater rocks. They swim by squirting water through their baglike bodies. As the water squirts out, the little octopus is pushed forward. Their eight wavy "arms," called tentacles, are lined with two rows of suckers. The babies use the suckers to hold on to food and to help them crawl.

BLUE WHALE

The baby blue whale lives in the ocean. It is the biggest baby in the world. When it is born, it can be 23 feet long. When fully grown, it can weigh as much as 24 elephants!

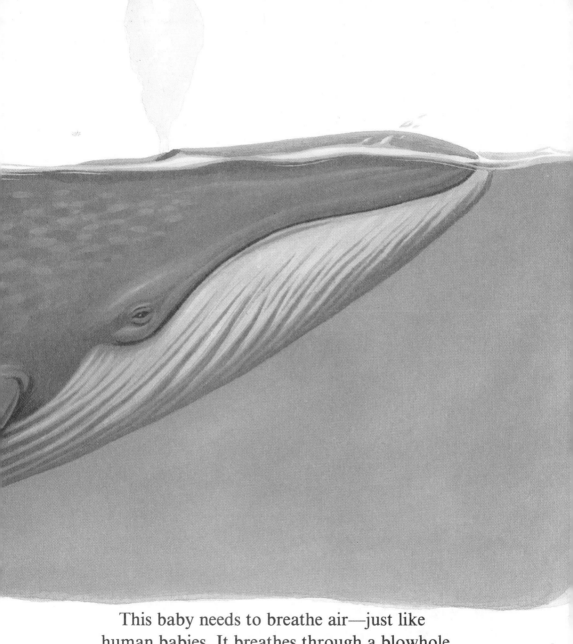

This baby needs to breathe air—just like
human babies. It breathes through a blowhole
on the top of its head. When the air is blown
out, it forms a misty spray called a spout.

HUMAN

Human babies can't swim. They have to learn how. Can you swim? If not, ask someone you know to teach you. Someday *you* may even feel at home in the water—just like the animal water babies.